QUICK & EASY
ELEGANT
PASTA

BARBARA RUSSO

JG
PRESS

Published by
World Publications, Inc.
455 Somerset Avenue
North Dighton, MA 02764

Produced by The Triangle Group, Ltd.
227 Park Avenue
Hoboken, NJ 07030

Editorial: Jake Elwell
Design: Tony Meisel
Printing: Cronion S.A., Barcelona

ISBN 1-57215-002-5

Printed in Spain

Contents

3

4

Introduction

Pasta has fast become everybody's favorite meal. It's quick, it's easy and it's liable to more variations than you can sample in a lifetime.

Pasta can be divided into two basic categories—fresh and dry. Additionally, it can be made with eggs or without. It can be stuffed as with tortellini or ravioli or plain as with spaghetti, linguini or penne. In either case, it is usually sauced.

Most Americans think that pasta is usually heavily sauced with tomato variations. In Italy, however, sauce is usually applied sparingly, so as not to drown the natural taste of the noodles themselves. And, depending where in the country one finds oneself, the sauces are often not made with tomatoes at all.

The great thing about pasta is that it is made up mainly of complex carbohydrates. Therefore, it is naturally healthy and not at all fattening by itself. The sauce makes the difference. Butter, cheese (and even the Italians often overdo the cheese), meats and sausages will naturally add many, many calories to any dish of pasta.

But sauces of fresh vegetables, fish, shellfish, olive oil and stock make refreshing, healthy and delicious dishes in their own right.

If the pasta is to be only a first course, be sure that what follows contrasts with the pasta, in taste and texture and substance. In other words, if one is going to eat tortellini with a meat sauce, a main course of grilled fish would be preferable to one of *stufato*, or pot roast.

Finally, a word about preparing pasta. Always cook it in a large amount of water. Always salt the water, otherwise the pasta will be insipid. And always drain it and sauce it immediately. People wait for pasta, pasta does not wait for people.

6 Spaghetti with Oil & Garlic

1 pound thin spaghetti
2 to 3 tablespoons olive oil
5-6 cloves or garlic, finely chopped
salt to taste
black pepper to taste

Cook the spaghetti in a large pot of salted boiling water. Drain.

In a small skillet heat the oil. Add the garlic and quickly sauté until the garlic begins to brown.

Place the spaghetti in a serving bowl. Add the garlic and oil, toss. Season with salt and pepper. Serves 4.

Elbows with Herbs & Cheese

1 pound elbow macaroni
1/2 cup low-fat margarine
2 cloves of garlic, crushed
2 tablespoons fresh basil, finely chopped
1 tablespoon fresh mint, finely chopped
1/4 cup grated Parmesan cheese
1/4 cup grated Romano cheese

Cook the pasta in a pot of salted boiling water. Drain.

While the pasta is cooking, melt the butter in a skillet; add the garlic, basil and mint. Sauté for 1-2 minutes.

Add the drained pasta to the skillet and mix well until covered with butter and herbs. Add the cheeses and mix gently but quickly. Season with fresh black pepper. Serve at once. Serves 4.

Spaghetti with Tomato Sauce | 7

1 pound spaghetti
2 tablespoons olive oil
3 cloves of garlic, finely chopped
2 pounds fresh tomatoes, chopped and seeded or 1 large can
    imported Italian tomatoes, drained
1/4 cup chopped fresh basil
1/4 cup chopped fresh arugula
2 tablespoons chopped parsley
salt to taste
black pepper to taste
freshly grated Parmesan cheese, optional

In a large skillet, heat the oil. Add the garlic and sauté for
1-2 minutes. Add the tomatoes and cook uncovered over a low
heat for 15-20 minutes or until the sauce begins to boil and
thicken. Keep hot.
    Cook the pasta in a pot of boiling salted water. Drain.
    Add the basil, arugula and parsley to the sauce. Stir well.
Place the pasta in a serving bowl. Toss with the sauce and season
to taste with salt and pepper. Sprinkle with cheese if desired.
Serves 4.

8

Spaghetti with
Oil & Garlic

9

Elbows with
Herbs & Cheese

10 | Pasta with Chicken Livers, Tomatoes & Garlic

1/2 pound fresh chicken livers
3 tablespoons olive oil
2 cloves garlic, peeled and chopped
1 large can imported Italian plum tomatoes, drained
1 teaspoon grated lemon peel
1 teaspoon fresh rosemary, chopped
2 tablespoons Marsala wine
1 pound bucatini or spaghetti
salt and pepper to taste

Clean the chicken livers and cut into small pieces.

Heat the olive oil in a saucepan and add the chopped garlic. Let brown lightly over medium heat. Add the tomatoes and mash roughly with the back of a wooden spoon. Add the lemon peel, rosemary, salt and pepper and let simmer for 15 minutes.

Cook the pasta in a pot of boiling salted water. Drain.

Just before serving add the Marsala to the sauce and simmer for 2 minutes. Pour over the drained pasta and serve immediately with grated Parmesan cheese on the side. Serves 4.

Rice Noodles with Peanut Sauce

This refreshing dish can be served as an appetizer or as part of an Oriental buffet. The fish sauce and noodles can be bought in larger supermarkets and Oriental shops.

8 ounce package of Oriental rice noodles
1 tablespoon sesame oil
2 cloves garlic, finely chopped
1 green pepper, cored, seeded and julienned
1 red pepper, cored, seeded and julienned
2 scallions, coarsely chopped
1 tablespoon fresh ginger, julienned
4-6 ounces small, cooked shrimp
2 tablespoons *nam phua* (Thai fish sauce)
1 tablespoon soy sauce
1/4 cup smooth peanut butter

Place noodles in a large bowl and cover with boiling water for 5 minutes. In a saucepan, heat the sesame oil. Sauté the garlic, peppers, scallions, ginger and shrimp for 5-7 minutes over high heat, tossing constantly. Add the fish sauce, soy sauce and peanut butter and toss well. Drain the noodles well and place in a bowl. Pour the shrimp and vegetable mixture over and serve. Serves 4.

12

Spaghetti with
Tomato Sauce

13

Pasta with
Chicken Livers,
Tomatoes & Garlic

14 | Macaroni & Cheese

The old stand-by with a new twist!

1 pound macaroni
3 tablespoons butter
3 tablespoons flour
2 cups warm 1% fat milk
1 cup grated low-fat cheddar cheese
1 teaspoon Tabasco sauce
1/2 teaspoon ground nutmeg
1 teaspoon black pepper
2 teaspoons salt

Boil the macaroni in at least 4 quarts of salted water until just firm. Drain and set aside. In a saucepan over low heat, melt the butter. Stir in the flour and blend thoroughly. Let cook 2 minutes. Slowly add the warm milk, stirring constantly, until well blended. Add the cheese and Tabasco and continue stirring until the cheese is melted and the whole mixture is smooth and thick. Place the macaroni in a deep, oven-proof casserole. Pour the cheese mixture over and fold in. Place in a 400 degree F. oven for 20 minutes until hot through and browned on top.
Serves 4.

Pasta with Tuna Sauce

An unusual combination, typical of the Ligurian coast of Northern Italy. It makes a fast, delicious meal, accompanied by a salad and dry white wine.

2 cloves garlic, chopped
1 7-ounce can tuna in olive oil
pulp from tomatoes
1 cup tomato juice made from Italian plum tomatoes
1/2 cup fresh basil leaves, finely chopped
1 teaspoon capers, roughly chopped
1 pound penne

First, make the sauce. Sauté garlic in the oil drained from the tuna. Add the tomato pulp and cook for two minutes over medium heat. Add the remaining ingredients, except the pasta and continue cooking for 10 minutes until well-blended and slightly reduced. Cook the penne in plenty of boiling, salted water until *al dente*, slightly resistant to the tooth. Drain pasta and immediately place in a heated, large bowl, add the sauce and toss thoroughly. Serve immediately. Serves 4.

Linguine with Clam Sauce

1/4 cup olive oil
1 medium onion, finely chopped
2 cloves of garlic, crushed
1 large can imported Italian tomatoes, drained, sieved
    and mixed with juices
1/2 teaspoon oregano
2 dashes of Tabasco sauce
2 dozen cherrystone clams, shucked and coarsely chopped,
    set aside in their juices
1 pound linguine

In a large skillet, heat the olive oil. Add the onions and sauté for 5 minutes or until the onions begin to wilt and become transparent. Add the garlic and cook 1 minute longer.

To the onion mixture add the tomatoes, oregano, and Tabasco; bring the mixture to a boil. Lower the heat to a simmer and continue cooking for 8-10 minutes or until the mixture begins to thicken and reduce.

Add the clams with their juices to the skillet cook over a low heat for 3-5 minutes.

Cook the linguine in a large pot of boiling salted water. Drain.

Transfer the linguine to a serving bowl and toss with some of the sauce. Spoon the rest of the sauce over the pasta. Serves 4.

16

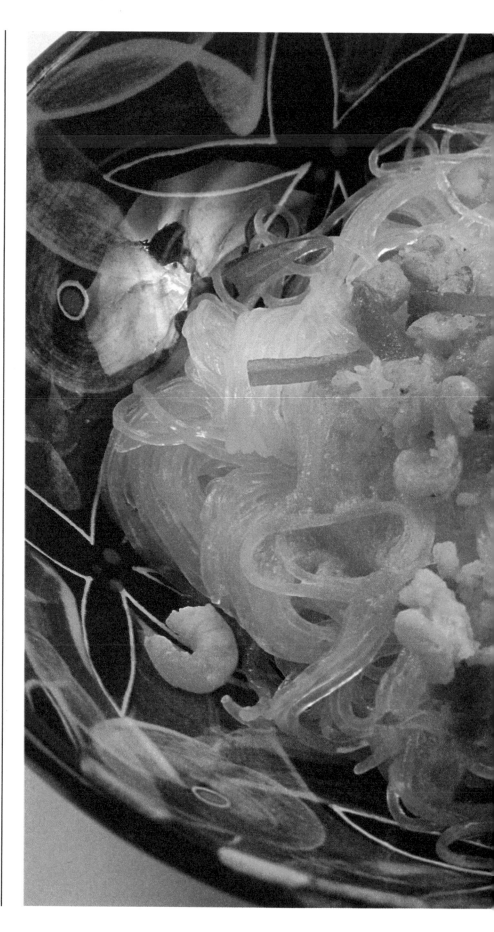

Rice Noodles with
Peanut-Ginger Sauce

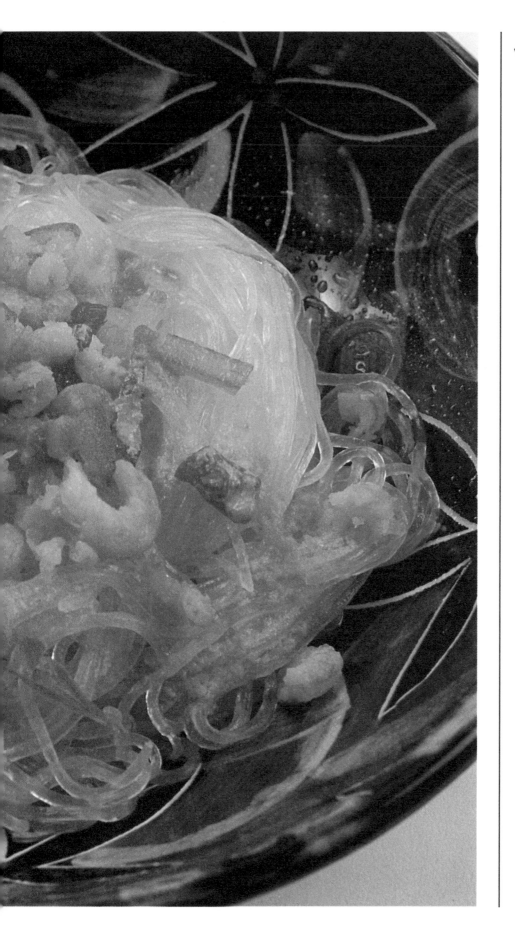

18 Spaghetti with Broccoli, Garlic & Oil

1 pound or 1 large bunch of broccoli
1/4 cup olive oil
4 cloves of garlic, finely chopped
1 pound spaghetti
freshly grated Parmesan cheese, to taste
black pepper, to taste

Cook the penne in a large pot of salted boiling water. Drain.

While the penne is cooking, trim the broccoli and break the bunch into florets. Steam 8-10 minutes or until just tender.

While the broccoli is cooking, heat the oil in a large skillet. Add the garlic and sauté briefly. When the broccoli is done, add it to the garlic oil mixture, sauté for 1-2 minutes.

Place the garlic and broccoli mixture in a large serving bowl. Add the penne and toss. Sprinkle with cheese and pepper to taste. Serves 4.

Spaghetti with Olives, Tomatoes & Anchovies

1/4 cup olive oil
2 cloves of garlic, finely chopped
1 can of anchovy fillets, finely chopped
1 large can of imported Italian tomatoes, drained and
    coarsely chopped, reserve juice
10-12 imported black olives, pitted and coarsely chopped
1/4 cup fresh basil, coarsely chopped
1 pound of spaghetti
black pepper to taste

In a large skillet heat the olive oil and stir in the garlic and anchovies. Cook until anchovies begin to disintegrate; about 2 minutes. Add the tomatoes and some of their juice, the olives and basil. Simmer the mixture over a medium heat, stirring occasionally, until the sauce thickens only slightly.

While the sauce is simmering, cook the spaghetti in a large pot of salted boiling water. Drain.

Transfer the spaghetti to a serving bowl and toss with the sauce. Season with pepper to taste. Serves 4.

Linguine with Seafood & Basil Cream

2 tablespoons butter
2 cloves garlic, peeled and chopped
1/2 pound shrimp, cleaned and deveined
1/2 pound scallops, cut in halves or quarters if large
1 cup fresh basil leaves, packed
1 teaspoon green peppercorns, crushed
1/2 cup light cream, heated
salt and pepper to taste
1 pound linguine

Cook the pasta in a large pot of boiling, salted water until *al dente*. Drain and serve with the following sauce.

In a skillet, melt the butter. Sauté garlic until lightly browned. Add the shrimp and scallops and cook over medium heat 5 minutes, until shrimp are pink and scallops opaque white. Add the basil, green peppercorns, hot cream and salt and pepper. Let simmer 5 minutes. Pour over pasta and serve immediately. Serves 4.

20

Pasta with
Tuna Sauce

22 | Twists with Chicken & Red Peppers

2 tablespoons olive oil
1 small onion, finely chopped
2 cloves garlic, peeled and chopped
1 whole chicken breast, skinned and
    cut into julienne strips
2 sweet red peppers, seeded, skinned and finely chopped
1/2 cup light cream
1/2 teaspoon Tabasco sauce
1 pound twists or any other short pasta

In a large skillet, sauté the onion and garlic in the olive oil. Add the chicken and cook over medium heat, stirring often, for 5 minutes until the chicken is lightly browned.

Add the red peppers and cook for another 5 minutes until soft and blended. Add the cream and Tabasco and simmer for 5 minutes more.

In the meantime, cook the pasta in boiling, salted water. Drain. Pour over the sauce, toss well and serve. Grated Romano cheese is a good addition. Serves 4.

Cannelloni

Cannelloni can be made from either of two types of pasta: dried, cooked, split and stuffed or with fresh pasta dough cut into rounds or squares, lightly cooked and then rolled-up like crêpes or pancakes. Either works well for this recipe.

1 onion, chopped
1 clove garlic, peeled and chopped
1/2 pound ground veal
2 anchovy filets, chopped
1 teaspoon capers, chopped
6 oil-cured black olives, pitted and chopped
1 tablespoon chopped fresh basil
1 tablespoon extra virgin olive oil
1 egg
8 cannelloni
2 cups light tomato sauce
1/2 cup Parmesan cheese, grated

In a large mixing bowl combine the onion, garlic, veal, anchovy, capers, olives, basil, olive oil and egg. Mix lightly yet thoroughly. Use this mixture to stuff the cannelloni.

Place the pasta tubes in a greased baking dish, cover with the tomato sauce and dust heavily with grated Parmesan cheese. Bake in a 400 degree F. oven for 20-25 minutes until the pasta is piping hot and the cheese is lightly browned. Serves 4.

24

Linguine with
Clam Sauce

Spaghetti with Broccoli,
Oil & Garlic

26 | Shells with Vodka Cream

1 pound pasta shells, large or small
1 tablespoon butter
1 clove garlic, peeled and chopped
1 tomato, peeled, seeded and chopped
1/4 pound shrimp, crushed into a paste
1/4 cup vodka
1/2 cup light cream
salt and pepper to taste

Cook the pasta shells in boiling, salted water until done. Drain.
Meanwhile, sauté the garlic in the butter in a skillet. Add the tomato and shrimp paste and cook for five minutes over medium heat, stirring constantly. Add the vodka and let cook for 2 minutes to evaporate the alcohol and blend the tastes. Finally, add the cream and simmer for 5 minutes. Pour over the pasta and serve. Serves 4.

Pasta Primavera

There are a thousand-and-one recipes for pasta primavera (spring-time pasta). The variety of vegetables depends entirely on what's available, but all should be young and in prime condition.

2 tablespoons butter or olive oil
2 cloves garlic, peeled and chopped
1 small onion, thinly sliced
1 cup mushrooms, thinly sliced
1 small zucchini, julienned
1 small carrot, julienned
1 cup broccoli flowerets
2 tomatoes, peeled, seeded and chopped
1 cup string beans, sliced lengthwise
1 cup asparagus tips
salt and pepper to taste
1 1/2 pounds linguini or other pasta

In a very large skillet or wok, heat the butter or olive oil (butter if to be eaten hot, olive oil to make into a salad).

Sauté the garlic, onions and mushrooms until soft and golden. Add all the other vegetables and toss over high heat until just crisp and hot. Pour over the cooked pasta and season with salt and pepper. Serve immediately

If you wish to make a salad to be served at room temperature, toss penne with vegetables, add another 1/2 cup of olive oil and vinegar to taste and let marinate for an hour before serving. Serves 6.

Tortellini with Ham & Peas

Excellent tortellini, filled with either meat or cheese, can be bought in most supermarkets and specialty food stores. This makes a very rich dish, perhaps best served as an appetizer before grilled fish or meat.

1 pound tortellini
1 tablespoon butter
1 cup fresh shelled peas
1/4 pound prosciutto or good baked ham, in julienne
2 tablespoons olive oil
1 teaspoon freshly ground black pepper

Cook the tortellini in gently boiling, salted water as per directions on the package.

Meanwhile, melt the butter in a small saucepan, add the peas, cover and cook over low heat for 10 minutes.

Uncover, add the ham and heat through, about 5 minutes. Finally, add the olive oil and heat to just the boiling point.

Pour over the hot tortellini, sprinkle with pepper and serve at once. Serves 4-6 as an appetizer.

28

Spaghetti with
Olives, Tomatoes
and Anchovies

30 | Pasta & Bean Soup

1 onion, finely chopped
1/4 pound bacon, diced
2 tablespoons olive oil
2 cloves garlic, chopped
4 cups chicken stock or canned broth
1 28-ounce can small cannellini beans
1 teaspoon hot pepper flakes
1/4 pound short pasta tubes

Sauté the onion and bacon in the olive oil, in a large saucepan adding the garlic after 3 minutes. Add the beans and pepper flakes and cook over low heat for 5 minutes stirring carefully (so as not to break the beans). Add the stock and simmer covered for 15 minutes.

   Finally, add the pasta and cook, uncovered until *al dente*, about 15 minutes more. Serves 4-6.

Spinach Pasta with Shrimp & Mushrooms

1/4 cup olive oil
3 cloves garlic, chopped
1/2 pound mushrooms, thinly sliced
1/2 pound shrimp, peeled, deveined and cut into quarters
1/4 cup dry white wine
1 tablespoon fresh basil, chopped
1 pound spinach pasta (linguine is ideal)

Sauté the garlic in the olive oil in a skillet until lightly browned. Add the mushrooms and cook over high heat just until the juices begin to emerge. Add the shrimp and cook for 5 minutes. Now add the white wine and basil and cook for 2 minutes more.

   Meanwhile, cook the pasta until *al dente* and drain.

   Pour the sauce over and serve immediately. Serves 4.

Spinach Fettucine with Mussels

4 pounds mussels, scrubbed and debearded
1 cup dry white wine
2 tablespoons olive oil
1 clove garlic, peeled and chopped
2 onion, peeled and sliced thinly
2 carrots, peeled and julienned
salt and pepper to taste
1 pound spinach fettucine

In a large pot, place the mussels and white wine. Steam in a covered pot, stirring occasionally, until the shells open. When cool enough to handle, shell the mussels, reserving a dozen in their shells for garnishing. Strain the liquid from the mussels through cheesecloth and reserve.

In a large saucepan, sauté the garlic and onion in the olive oil until soft and golden. Add the carrot and cook gently, until soft. Season with salt and pepper. Add the shelled mussels and just enough of the reserved liquid to moisten everything to a depth of about 1 inch. Heat through, but do not let boil or the mussels will toughen.

Meanwhile, cook the fettucine in boiling, salted water until done. Drain.

Pour the sauce over the pasta and toss well. Garnish with the reserved mussels in their shells. Serves 4.

Linguine with Seafood
and Basil Cream

Twists with Chicken
& Red Peppers

34 | Rigatoni Siciliana

1/4 cup olive oil
2 cloves garlic, peeled and chopped
1 medium eggplant, peeled and cut into 1/2 inch cubes
1 28-ounce can plum tomatoes, drained and coarsely chopped
1/2 cup seedless white raisins
1/2 teaspoon red pepper flakes
1 pound rigatoni

In a large skillet, sauté the garlic in the olive oil over medium heat. Add the eggplant and continue cooking, stirring constantly, for 5 minutes until the eggplant is softened. Add the tomatoes and cook for 15 minutes.

Meanwhile, soak the raisins in hot water for 10 minutes. Drain.

Add the raisins and the red pepper flakes to the sauce and cook for five minutes more.

Cook the rigatoni in boiling, salted water until *al dente*. Drain. Pour the sauce over and serve. Serves 4.

Ravioli Siciliana

This rather bizarre-sounding dish is actually quite good and mingles the flavors of Italy with the Arab-influenced cuisine of Sicily.

2 tablespoons pine nuts
2 tablespoons olive oil
1 large onion, peeled and chopped
2 cloves garlic peeled and chopped
1 28-ounce can plum tomatoes, drained and chopped
1 large can skinless, boneless sardines, preferably in olive oil, drained and coarsely chopped
1/2 cup seedless white raisins, soaked for 10 minutes in hot water and drained
1 teaspoon hot red pepper flakes
1 pound small cheese-stuffed ravioli (available fresh at many markets and specialty stores)

Place the pine nuts on a baking sheet and toast for 10 minutes in a medium oven. Remove, cool and set aside.

In a large skillet, sauté the onion and garlic in the olive oil over medium heat, until soft and golden. Add the tomatoes and simmer, stirring occasionally, for 10 minutes. Add the sardines, raisins and red pepper flakes and simmer for 10 minutes more.

Meanwhile cook the ravioli as per the instructions on the package. Drain. Top with the sauce and serve immediately. Serves 4.

Pasta with Spinach & Sausages

1 tablespoon butter
1 clove garlic, peeled and chopped
1/2 pound sweet or hot low-fat Italian sausage,
    removed from the casings
1 10-ounce package frozen chopped spinach, defrosted
1/2 cup light cream
1 pound bucatini or penne

Sauté the garlic in the butter in a large skillet. When lightly browned, add the sausage meat and cook over medium heat, breaking up the sausage with a fork until lightly browned and almost reduced to sausage crumbs.

Add the spinach and mix well. Add the cream and let heat through.

Meanwhile, cook the pasta in boiling, salted water. Drain.

Toss the pasta well with the sauce and serve at once. Serves 4.

36

Cannelloni

Shells with
Vodka Cream

38 | Orzo with Nuts & Mushrooms

Orzo is the tiny, grain-shaped pasta. It cooks very quickly and is perfect as a side-dish, to accompany roast or grilled meats.

4 tablespoons butter
1 clove garlic, peeled and chopped
1/2 pound mushrooms, roughly chopped
2 tablespoons walnuts or pecans, coarsely chopped
pepper to taste
1 pound orzo

Melt the butter in a large skillet. Sauté the garlic and mushrooms until soft and lightly browned. Add the chopped nuts and heat through.

Meanwhile, cook the orzo in boiling, salted water. This should only take about 5 minutes. Drain.

Toss the orzo with the sauce. Serves 4.

Rigatoni with Ragout

This is a dish to make when you are cooking a stew or pot roast (especially if flavored with red wine and herbs).

3 cups gravy from stew or pot roast
1 pound rigatoni
1/2 cup grated Parmesan cheese

Place the gravy in a small saucepan and cook over low heat, uncovered, for at least 1 hour, until the gravy is reduced to half its original volume.

Meanwhile, cook the rigatoni in boiling, salted water. Drain.

Toss the pasta with the gravy and 1/2 cup of grated Parmesan cheese. Serve more cheese on the side. Serves 4.

Pasta-Shrimp Salad

1 pound medium shrimp, peeled and deveined
1 cup fresh raw peas
1 tablespoon chopped pimentos
3/4 cup extra virgin olive oil
2 tablespoon wine vinegar
2 teaspoons Dijon mustard
salt and pepper to taste
1 pound penne or ziti, cooked and drained

Cook the shrimp in boiling, salted water for 3 minutes. Drain.
    Toss the shrimp with the peas, pimentos, olive oil, vinegar
mustard and salt and pepper to taste.
    Add the pasta and toss well. Serve at room temperature.
Serves 4-6.

Farfalle with Peas & Bacon

1/4 pound pancetta or lightly smoked bacon, diced
1 clove garlic, peeled and chopped
1 cup fresh peas, shelled
3/4 cup chicken broth
pepper to taste
1/2 cup grated Parmesan cheese
1 pound farfalle

In a skillet fry the pancetta or bacon until the fat runs. Add the
garlic, peas and chicken broth and cook over a low heat for
15 minutes, until the peas are tender and the broth has reduced.
    In the meantime, cook the farfalle in boiling, salted water until
al dente. Drain.
    Pour the sauce over the pasta, add pepper to taste
and Parmesan cheese. Toss well. Serves 4.

Pasta Primavera

42 | Penne with Pesto

Pesto is the wonderful, uncooked sauce of Genoa and the Ligurian coast. There are dozens of recipes; all I can say is this one is authentic and good.

1 large bunch fresh basil
2-3 cloves garlic, peeled
1/4 cup pine nuts
1/4 cup Parmesan cheese or Parmesan and Romano mixed
1/2 cup extra virgin olive oil
pepper to taste
1 pound penne
1/4 cup melted butter

Place the basil (leaves only), garlic, pine nuts and cheese in a food processor. Cover. Process, slowly adding the olive oil until a thick paste is achieved. Add pepper to taste.

In the meantime, cook the penne in boiling, salted water until *al dente*. Drain and toss with the melted butter. Place a spoonful of the pesto on each portion and serve with more cheese and butter. Each person mixes his or her own at the table. Serves 4.

Orechiette with Sausage

Orechiette—little ears—are a delightful form of pasta for hearty, peasant-like dishes. They stand up well to strong flavors.

1/4 cup olive oil
1/2 pound hot low-fat Italian sausage, skinned and broken up
1 clove garlic, peeled and chopped
1/4 cup dry white wine
1 large ripe tomato, peeled, seeded and roughly chopped
1 pound orechiette

In a large skillet, heat the olive oil. Add the sausage and garlic and let sauté for about 10 minutes, until the sausage bits are cooked through. Add the white wine and let simmer for 5 minutes to reduce and thicken.

In the meantime, cook the pasta in boiling, salted water until *al dente*. Drain.

Toss the pasta with the sauce. Sprinkle the raw tomato over the top. Serves 4.

44

Tortellini with
Ham & Peas

45

Ravioli Siciliana

46 | Ham & Vegetable Pasta Salad

A good way to use leftover ham and an excellent summer-time main course. Serve this salad with a German Mosel or Rhine white wine.

1 pound pasta shapes, cooked
2 tablespoons extra virgin olive oil
1 cup fresh peas
1 cup raw carrots, sliced
1 cup broccoli florets
1 cup cooked ham, cubed
1/4 cup grated Parmesan cheese
2 tablespoons fresh parsley, chopped
1 1/4 cup Italian Dressing
1 teaspoon freshly ground black pepper

Put the cooked pasta in a salad bowl and add the olive oil. Toss to coat the pasta well. Cook the peas, carrots and broccoli in a large pan of boiling water until just tender, about 8-10 minutes. Drain and rinse with cold water. Drain again. Add the vegetables, ham, cheese and parsley to the pasta. Toss until well mixed. Add the Italian Dressing and lightly toss. Serves 6.

Linguine Salad

This makes a perfect impromptu luncheon salad for those unexpected summertime guests.

4 large tomatoes, seeded and coarsely chopped
1/4 cup marinated artichoke hearts, drained and chopped
4 teaspoons parsley, chopped
1 cup Italian Dressing
1 teaspoon Tabasco sauce
1 pound linguine

Put the tomatoes, artichoke hearts and parsley in a salad bowl. Add the Tabasco sauce to the Italian Dressing and pour over the tomatoes and artichoke hearts. Let stand at room temperature for one hour. Cook the linguine in large pot of boiling water until just tender. Drain well and add the linguine to the salad bowl. Toss well and serve. Serves 4-6

Fusilli with Basil

1 cup chopped fresh basil leaves
1 teaspoon chopped garlic
1/2 cup pitted black olives in brine, drained and chopped
1 pound tomatoes, skinned and chopped
1/2 cup extra virgin olive oil
1 teaspoon black pepper
1 pound fusilli

Mix all ingredients but the fusilli together in a bowl and let stand for 1 hour.

Boil the fusilli in plenty of salted water until *al dente*. Drain. Toss with the uncooked sauce and serve immediately. Serves 4.

48

Pasta & Bean Soup

50 | Manicotti Crêpes

1 cup cottage cheese or ricotta
1 3-ounce package cream cheese, softened
2 tablespoons butter, softened
2 tablespoons chopped fresh parsley
1 egg, beaten
1 tablespoon chopped scallions
8 cooked crêpes
2 cups tomato sauce
2 teaspoons fresh parsley, chopped
2 teaspoons dried oregano
2 teaspoons dried basil
1/2 teaspoon chopped garlic
1/4 cup Parmesan cheese

Combine the first six ingredients. Spoon 3 tablespoons of this mixture into the center of each crepe. Combine the sauce with the parsley, oregano, basil and garlic. Place the filled crêpes in a shallow baking pan and pour the sauce over them. Sprinkle with Parmesan cheese. Bake at 350 degrees for 20-30 minutes. Serves 4.

BASIC CRÊPES
2 fresh eggs at room temperature
1 cup milk
1 cup flour
1 tablespoon melted butter

In blender mix together the eggs and milk for 30 seconds. Keeping speed on low, slowly add the flour and butter, just until blended. Grease lightly a 7" skillet. Pour a scant 1/4 cup of batter on the pan. Tilt the pan so batter spreads evenly. Brown the bottom of the crêpe lightly and remove from the pan when the top becomes dry.

Linguine with Nasturtium Flowers

Nasturtium flowers have a sharp, peppery tang that makes them the perfect foil for oil, garlic and cheese.

1 cup shredded nasturtium flowers
2 cloves garlic, finely chopped
1 cup finely shredded arugula leaves
1/2 cup virgin olive oil
1 pound linguine
1/2 cup grated Romano cheese

Sauté the nasturtium flowers, garlic and arugula in the olive oil for 5 minutes.

Cook the linguine in boiling, salted water until *al dente*. Drain. Pour the sauce over and toss with Romano cheese. Serves 4.

Spinach Pasta with
Shrimp & Mushrooms

54 | Ham-Asparagus Crêpes

8 crepes
8 slices lean ham
16 spears asparagus, cooked
Tarragon Hollandaise Sauce

Place one slice of lean ham on the unbrowned side of the crêpe. Place 2 spears of cooked asparagus, end to end, on the ham. Roll to form a cigar-shaped crêpe. Tips of asparagus should show outside the crêpe. Warm at 300 degrees for 15 minutes. Serve with tarragon hollandaise sauce. Serves 4.

TARRAGON HOLLANDAISE SAUCE

1/2 cup butter
2 egg yolks, well beaten
1 tablespoon lemon juice
1 teaspoon dried tarragon

Divide the butter into 3 portions. Put egg yolks and 1/3 of the butter into top of a double boiler over hot water. Beat constantly with a wire whisk. When butter melts, add another portion. As the mixture thickens add the remaining 1/3 butter. Remove from heat and add the lemon juice and tarragon. Serve immediately.

Pasta with Lemon-Olive Meatballs

1 pound ground beef
3 tablespoons lemon juice
1 tablespoon herb salt
1 1/2 cups Romano cheese, grated
12 black olives, pitted and finely chopped
1/4 green pepper, finely chopped
1/2 cup fine bread crumbs
1 egg
1/4 cup milk
1/4 cup olive oil
1 pound pasta
Parmesan cheese, grated

Mix together the beef, lemon juice and herb salt. Add the grated cheese, olives, pepper, bread crumbs, milk and egg. Shape into small balls and sauté in the olive oil. In the meantime cook the pasta in plenty of salted boiling water until done. Drain and pour the meatballs over the pasta in a hot serving dish. Pass the cheese separately. Serves. 4.

Rigatoni Siciliana

58 | Bucatini With Bacon, Onion & Red Pepper

4 tablespoons olive oil
1/2 pound pancetta or smoked bacon, cut in matchstick lengths
1 large, sweet onion, finely chopped
1 teaspoon hot red pepper flakes
1 pound bucatini
grated Parmesan cheese
black pepper

Heat the olive oil in a large sauté pan. Add the pancetta or bacon and the onion and cook over moderate heat for 10 minutes.

Meanwhile, cook the bucatini in a large pot of boiling, salted water until *al dente*. Drain

Pour the bacon-onion mixture over the pasta and toss well, adding Parmesan and pepper to taste. Serves 4.

Linguine with Fresh Tomatoes

2 tablespoons olive oil
3 cloves garlic, peeled and chopped
3 pounds plum tomatoes, peeled, seeded and roughly chopped
2 tablespoons fresh basil, finely chopped
black pepper to taste
1 pound linguine

Heat the olive oil in a large skillet. Add the garlic and let cook over moderate heat for 2 minutes. Add the tomatoes, cover the pan and cook gently for 15 minutes. Add the basil.

Meanwhile, cook the linguine in a large pot of boiling, salted water until *al dente*. Drain

Pour the sauce over the pasta and sprinkle with black pepper. Serves 4.

Orechiette with Olives & Anchovies

This is a salty, lusty dish. Have plenty of wine on hand.

4 tablespoons olive oil
1 tablespoon chopped garlic
1/2 pound brine-cured black olives, pitted and roughly chopped
1 small tin anchovy filets with oil, roughly chopped
10-ounce package, frozen, chopped spinach, defrosted
1 teaspoon black pepper
1 pound orechiette

In a large pan, sauté the garlic in the olive oil for 2 minutes. Add the olives and anchovies with their oil and let cook over low heat for 10 minutes. Add the defrosted spinach and let cook covered for 5 minutes.

Meanwhile, cook the orechiette in a large pot of boiling, salted water until *al dente*. This will take longer than with most pasta, about 15-20 minutes. Drain.

Pour the sauce over the pasta and serve immediately. No cheese. Serves 4.

Spinach Fettucine
with Mussels

62 | Pasta with Fennel & Sausage

2 large bulbs fennel
1 cup chicken stock
juice of 1 lemon
2 tablespoons butter
1 teaspoon salt
1 teaspoon black pepper
2 tablespoons olive oil
1 pound sweet Italian sausages, casings removed
1 pound pasta
grated Asiago cheese

Trim the fennel bulbs and finely shred. In a small casserole place the fennel, stock, lemon juice, butter, salt and pepper. Cover the casserole and bake in a 325 degree F. oven for 30 minutes.

Heat the olive oil in a large pan and sauté the sausage meat, broken up, until all traces of pink disappear and the meat is lightly browned. Remove the fennel from the oven and add it to the sausage in the pan. Continue to cook for 10 minutes over low heat until some of the broth is reduced and the flavors are blended.

Meanwhile, cook the pasta in a large pot of boiling, salted water until *al dente*. Drain.

Pour the sauce over the pasta, toss well, adding cheese as desired. Serves 4.

Clam & Pasta Salad

1/2 pound pasta, cooked and drained
1/2 cup extra virgin olive oil
1/2 pound cooked clams, chopped
3 tablespoons fresh lemon juice
1 1/2 garlic cloves, minced
3 tablespoons fresh parsley, chopped
2 tablespoons fresh basil, chopped
1 tablespoon fresh mint, chopped
3 tablespoons freshly grated Parmesan cheese
1/2 teaspoon salt
1 teaspoon freshly ground black pepper

Put the pasta in a large salad bowl and add one tablespoon of the olive oil. Lightly toss, add the clams and toss again. Put the remaining olive oil, lemon juice and garlic in a jar with a tightly fitting lid. Cover and shake until well mixed. Add the parsley, basil, mint, Parmesan cheese, salt and pepper. Shake again until blended. Pour the dressing over the salad and toss again. Serve at once or chill up to two hours before serving. Serves 4-6.

64

Pasta with
Spinach & Sausages

66 Spaghetti with Zucchini

2 tablespoons olive oil
4 tablespoons butter
1 pound very small zucchini, unpeeled and thinly sliced
2 cloves garlic, finely chopped
2 tablespoons cilantro, finely chopped
1 teaspoon black pepper
1 pound spaghetti
grated Parmesan cheese

In a saucepan, heat the olive oil and butter. Add the zucchini and toss to coat with the butter and oil. Cover and simmer for 15 minutes.

Meanwhile, cook the spaghetti in a large pot of boiling, salted water until *al dente*. Drain.

Add the garlic, cilantro and pepper to the zucchini and cook another 5 minutes. Pour the sauce over the pasta and add Parmesan to taste. Serves 4.

Shells with Mascarpone & Walnuts

2 tablespoons butter
8 ounces mascarpone or other double cream cheese
1/4 cup grated Parmesan cheese
1/4 cup walnuts, finely chopped
freshly ground black pepper to taste
1 pound pasta shells

Melt the butter in a fireproof serving dish. Add the mascarpone and heat very gently. Do not allow it to boil.

Meanwhile, cook the shells in a large pot of boiling, salted water until *al dente*. Drain.

Add the shells to the cheese and butter mixture and toss well. Add the Parmesan and walnuts and pepper and toss again. Serves 4.

Pasta with Ricotta

1/2 pound fresh ricotta
1/4 cup grated Parmesan cheese
2 tablespoons butter
1/2 teaspoon ground nutmeg
1/2 teaspoon salt
1 /2 teaspoon black pepper
1 pound pasta

In a bowl, whip the ricotta with a fork until smooth. Add the Parmesan, butter, nutmeg, salt and pepper and stir until well-blended.

Meanwhile, cook the pasta in a large pot of boiling, salted water until *al dente*. Drain.

Toss the cheese mixture with the pasta in a heatproof dish and place in a moderate oven for 10 minutes, until the cheese heats through and softens. Serves 4.

Pasta with Artichoke Sauce

10-ounce package frozen artichoke hearts, defrosted
1/2 cup chicken stock
1/4 cup grated carrot
1/2 cup heavy cream
1/2 teapsoon ground allspice
1 teaspoon black pepper
2 tablespoons butter
1 pound pasta

Place the artichoke hearts and stock in a covered saucepan and steam until the artichokes are soft. Purée in a food processor and return to the saucepan.

Add the carrot, cream, allspice and pepper to the artichoke puré and heat gently.

Meanwhile, cook the pasta in a large pot of boiling, salted water until *al dente*. Drain.

Toss the pasta with the sauce and serve immediately. Serves 4.

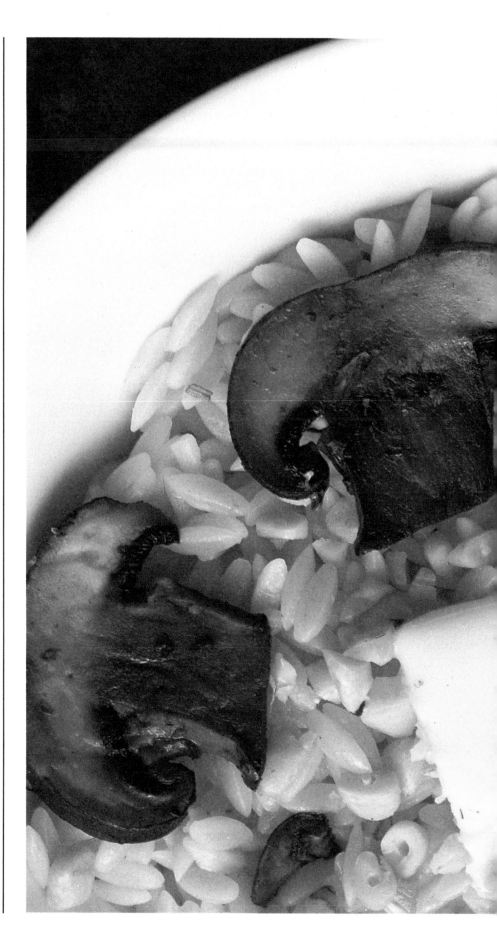

68

Orzo with
Nuts & Mushrooms

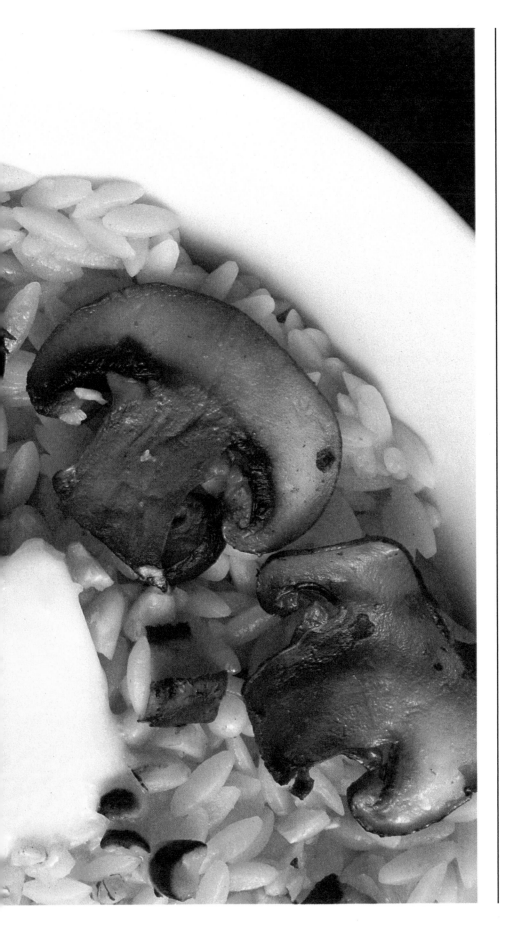

70 | Curried Orzo

2 tablespoons butter
1 large onion, chopped
1 small tart apple, peeled, cored and chopped
2-3 tablespoons curry paste (or powder)
1 teaspoon powdered ginger
1/2 teaspoon ground coriander
1 cup chicken, shrimp or pork, cooked and chopped (optional)
1 pound orzo

In a saucepan, sauté the onion in the butter. When soft and transparent add the apple, curry paste, ginger and coriander and cook for 10 minutes over moderate heat.

Add the meat if you are using it and let heat through.

Meanwhile, cook the orzo in a large pot of boiling, salted water until *al dente*. Drain.

Serve the curry spooned over the orzo. Serves 4.

Spaghetti with Red Peppers & Capers

3 tablespoons olive oil
2 cloves garlic, chopped
2 large sweet red peppers, peeled, seeded and cut into thin strips
1/2 cup dry red wine
1 tablespoon capers, rinsed
1/2 cup fresh parsley, finely chopped
1 pound thin spaghetti

In a large pan, heat the olive oil. Add the garlic and red peppers and sauté for 10 minutes over medium heat.

Meanwhile, cook the spaghetti in a large pot of boiling, salted water until *al dente*. Drain.

Add the red wine, turn up the heat and cook for 5 minutes until the wine is reduced and syrupy. Add the capers and pour over the spaghetti. Serves 4.

Rotelle with Bacon & Onions

1 tablespoon butter
1/4 pound bacon, cut into match sticks
2 large, sweet onions, very thinly sliced
1 teaspoon hot red pepper flakes
1/2 cup grated Romano cheese

Melt the butter in a large pan. Add the bacon strips and cook over medium heat until the bacon starts to give up its fat and lightly browns.

Add the onions and cook, stirring, for 15 minutes until the onions are soft and transparent.

Meanwhile, cook the rotelle in a large pot of boiling, salted water until *al dente*. Drain.

Add the red pepper flakes to the onion mixture and pour over the rotelle. Toss well with the cheese. Serves 4.

Rigatoni with Ragout

74 | Farfalle with Peas & Cream

1/2 pound fresh peas (weight after shelling)
1/2 cup chicken stock
1/2 teaspoon garlic, finely chopped
3/4 cup light cream
1 tablespoon butter
1 cup leftover chicken or pork, shredded (optional)
salt and pepper to taste
1/3 cup grated Parmesan cheese
1 pound farfalle

In a medium saucepan, cook the peas with the stock, covered, for 5 minutes. Drain the peas, reserving the stock. Return the stock to the pot and reduce by one-half.

Meanwhile, cook the farfalle in a large pot of boiling, salted water until *al dente*. Drain.

Add the peas, cream, butter, meat (if you are using it) and salt and pepper to taste. Let heat through and toss with the farfalle and the cheese. Serves 4.

Note: 1 tablespoon of fresh herbs—parsley, chervil, tarragon, mint—alone or in combination can be added to the sauce when you add the cream.

Penne with Roe

4 tablespoons butter
1 clove garlic, finely chopped
1/2 pound fresh shad, flounder or salmon roe,
    removed from membranes
1/2 cup Italian parsley, finely chopped
1/2 cup light cream (optional)
black pepper
1 pound penne

In a pan, melt the butter. Add the garlic and roe, and cook very gently for 5 minutes.

Meanwhile, cook the penne in a large pot of boiling, salted water until *al dente*. Drain.

Add the parsley and cream and heat through. Season with freshly ground black pepper. Serves 4.

Linguine with Tuna & Red Wine

1 7-ounce can tuna in olive oil
1 large onion, peeled and thinly sliced
2 cloves garlic, finely chopped
1/2 teaspoon dried oregano
1/2 cup dry red wine
1 pound linguine

In a large pan, place the tuna with its oil, the onion, garlic and oregano. Cover and cook slowly for 20 minutes.

Add the red wine to the pan and reduce, over medium heat, for 10 minutes.

Meanwhile, cook the linguine in a large pot of boiling, salted water until *al dente*. Drain.

Pour the sauce over the pasta and toss well. Serves 4.

Pasta-Shrimp Salad

78 | Shells with Lobster Salad

1 cup cooked lobster meat
2 tablespoons onion, finely chopped
2 tablespoons sweet vermouth
6 tablespoons virgin olive oil
1 tablespoon wine vinegar
2 teaspoons fresh tarragon, finely chopped
1/2 teaspoon Tabasco sauce
salt and pepper to taste
1 pound medium shells

In a large salad bowl, mix all the ingredients except the shells.

Meanwhile, cook the shells in a large pot of boiling, salted water until *al dente*. Drain.

Mix the warm shells with the lobster mixture. Serve at room temperature. Serves 4-6.

Orzo with Crab & Asparagus

2 tablespoons olive oil
1/2 pound fresh crab meat
1/2 teaspoon red pepper flakes
3/4 cup light cream
1 cup asparagus tips and stems, cut into 1-inch pieces
salt and pepper to taste
1/4 cup grated Parmesan cheese
1 pound orzo

In a large pan, heat the olive oil. Add the crab, red pepper, cream and asparagus and cook gently for 10 minutes.

Meanwhile, cook the orzo in a large pot of boiling, salted water until *al dente*. Drain.

Toss the sauce with the orzo, adding the cheese and salt and pepper to taste. Serves 4.

Spaghetti with Dried Tomatoes

1/2 cup dried tomatoes in oil, cut in strips and with their oil
1 onion, peeled and chopped
1/2 cup celery, chopped
1/2 cup carrot, chopped
2 cloves garlic, finely chopped
1 large can plum tomatoes, with juice
1/3 cup dry white wine
1 teaspoon dried fennel seed
black pepper to taste
1 pound spaghetti
3/4 cup grated Parmesan cheese

Heat the oil from the dried tomatoes in a large saucepan. Add the onion, celery, carrots and garlic and sauté for 15 minutes, stirring occasionally.

Stir in the dried and canned tomatoes, wine, fennel seeds and pepper. Simmer for 1/2 hour, stirring occasionally.

Meanwhile, cook the spaghetti in a large pot of boiling, salted water until *al dente*. Drain.

Pour the sauce into the bowl of a food processor and process for 15 seconds or until you have a chunky purée. Pour over pasta and pass cheese separately. Serves 4.

80

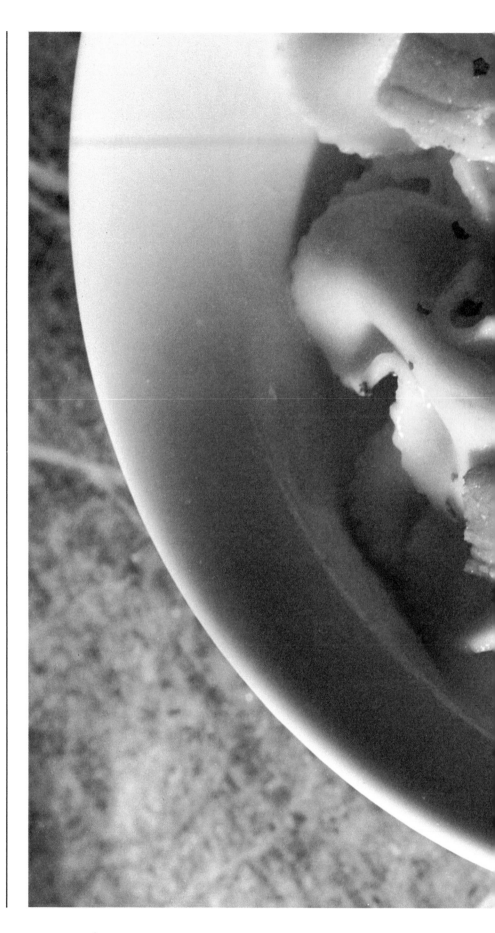

Farfalle with
Peas & Bacon

82 | Angel Hair with Feta & Prosciutto

2 tablespoons butter
1 tablespoon olive oil
1 clove garlic, finely chopped
1/2 cup prosciutto, chopped
3/4 cup feta cheese, crumbled
3/4 cup chicken stock
black pepper to taste
1 pound angel hair pasta

In a large saucepan, melt the butter and oil together. Add the garlic and sauté for 2 minutes. Now add the prosciutto and cook for 5 minutes more.

Meanwhile, cook the angel hair in a large pot of boiling, salted water until *al dente*. (Warning: it cooks very fast!) Drain.

Add the feta, chicken stock and pepper to the prosciutto and cook for 2 minutes.

Pour immediately over the angel hair and serve at once. Serves 4.

Pasta with Escarole & Veal

3 tablespoons olive oil
2 cloves garlic, finely chopped
1/2 pound lean veal, ground
1 pound escarole, washed and shredded
1/2-3/4 cup chicken stock
salt and black pepper to taste
1 pound pasta

In a large pan, heat the olive oil. Add the garlic and veal, and cook over high heat for 3-4 minutes, stirring constantly. Add the escarole, stock, salt and pepper and lower the heat. Cook for 15 minutes, until the stock is reduced by half.

Meanwhile, cook the pasta in a large pot of boiling, salted water until *al dente*. Drain.

Toss the sauce with the pasta. Serves 4.

Ham & Vegetable
Pasta Salad

86 | Rigatoni with Chicken & Mushrooms

4 tablespoons butter
2 cloves garlic, finely chopped
1/2 pound mushrooms, thinly sliced
1 cup leftover chicken, shredded
3/4 cup light cream
1/2 teaspoon black pepper
2 tablespoons parsley, finely chopped
1 pound rigatoni
grated Parmesan cheese

In a large pan, melt the butter. Add the garlic and let cook over moderate heat for 2 minutes. Add the mushrooms and cook for 10 minutes until soft.

Meanwhile, cook the pasta in a large pot of boiling, salted water until *al dente*. Drain.

Now add the chicken, cream, pepper and parsley and let simmer for 5 minutes until heated through. Pour over the pasta and pass cheese separately. Serves 4.

Angel Hair &
Spicy Tomatoes

A truly quick dish for those harried days. Serve with crusty bread and a green salad.

2 tablespoons olive oil
1 teaspoon garlic, chopped
1 small onion, peeled and sliced
1 large can plum tomatoes
1 tablespoon fresh basil, chopped
1 teaspoon Tabasco sauce
1 pound angel hair pasta

In a large pan, sauté the garlic and onion in the olive oil until soft. Add the tomatoes, with their juice, turn up the heat, and reduce to desired thickness.

Meanwhile, cook the pasta in a large pot of boiling, salted water until *al dente*. Drain.

Add the basil and Tabasco and cook for 2 minutes. Toss with the pasta. Serves 4.

88

Orechiette
with Sausage

Penne with Pesto

90 Spinach Fettucine with Herbed Cauliflower

1 head cauliflower, trimmed and cut into flowerets
2 tablespoons olive oil
1/2 cup chicken stock
1 tablesppon fresh parsley, finely chopped
1 teaspoon dried oregano
1/2 teaspoon dried thyme
1/2 teaspoon black pepper
grated Romano cheese
1 pound spinach fettucine

Steam the cauliflower in a small amount of salted water in a covered pot until just firm to the bite. Drain.

Meanwhile, cook the pasta in a large pot of boiling, salted water until *al dente*. Drain.

In a large pan, sauté the cauliflower in the olive oil until lightly browned. Add the stock, herbs and pepper, and simmer for 2 minutes. Pour over the pasta and pass cheese separately. Serves 4.

Pasta with Calamari

3 tablespoons olive oil
1 onion, thinly sliced
1 pound calamari, cleaned and cut into thin rings
1 large can plum tomatoes, drained and roughly chopped
1/4 cup wine vinegar
1 teaspoon dried oregano
1/2 teaspoon hot pepper flakes
1/2 teaspoon black pepper
1 teaspoon salt
1 pound pasta

In a large pan, heat the olive oil. Sauté the onion until soft and transparent. Add the calamari and cook gently for 5 minutes.

Add the tomatoes, vinegar, oregano, hot pepper, pepper and salt. Cover and simmer for 20 minutes until the calamari is tender.

Meanwhile, cook the pasta in a large pot of boiling, salted water until *al dente*. Drain.

Pour the sauce over the pasta. Serves 4.

Note: Pasta with seafood sauces are rarely, if ever, served with cheese in Italy.

Pasta Machine